LEVERS

Jennifer Howse

www.av2books.com

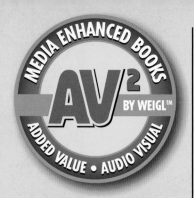

AV² provides enriched content that supplements and complements this book. Weigl's AV² books strive to create inspired learning and engage young minds in a total learning experience.

Your AV² Media Enhanced books come alive with...

Audio
Listen to sections of the book read aloud.

Key Words
Study vocabulary, and complete a matching word activity.

Go to **www.av2books.com**, and enter this book's unique code.

Video
Watch informative video clips.

Quizzes
Test your knowledge.

BOOK CODE

S772710

Embedded Weblinks
Gain additional information for research.

Slide Show
View images and captions, and prepare a presentation.

AV² by Weigl brings you media enhanced books that support active learning.

Try This!
Complete activities and hands-on experiments.

... and much, much more!

Published by AV² by Weigl
350 5th Avenue, 59th Floor
New York, NY 10118

Website: www.av2books.com   www.weigl.com

Library of Congress Cataloging-in-Publication Data

Howse, Jennifer.
 Levers / Jennifer Howse.
   p. cm. -- (Simple machines)
 Summary: "Presents information on simple machines with a focus on levers. Explains what a lever is, how levers work, and includes examples of past and present uses. Intended for third to fifth grade students"--Provided by publisher.
 Includes index.
 ISBN 978-1-62127-425-4 (hardcover : alk. paper) -- ISBN 978-1-62127-431-5 (softcover : alk. paper)
 1. Levers--Juvenile literature. I. Title.
 TJ147.H73 2013
 621.8'11--dc23
                          2012041019

Printed in the United States of America in North Mankato, Minnesota
1 2 3 4 5 6 7 8 9 0 17 16 15 14 13

042013
WEP040413

Project Coordinator: Alexis Roumanis
Design: Mandy Christiansen

Photo Credits
Weigl acknowledges Getty Images as the primary photo supplier for this title. Page 8, Alamy. Page 22, A. R. Roumanis.

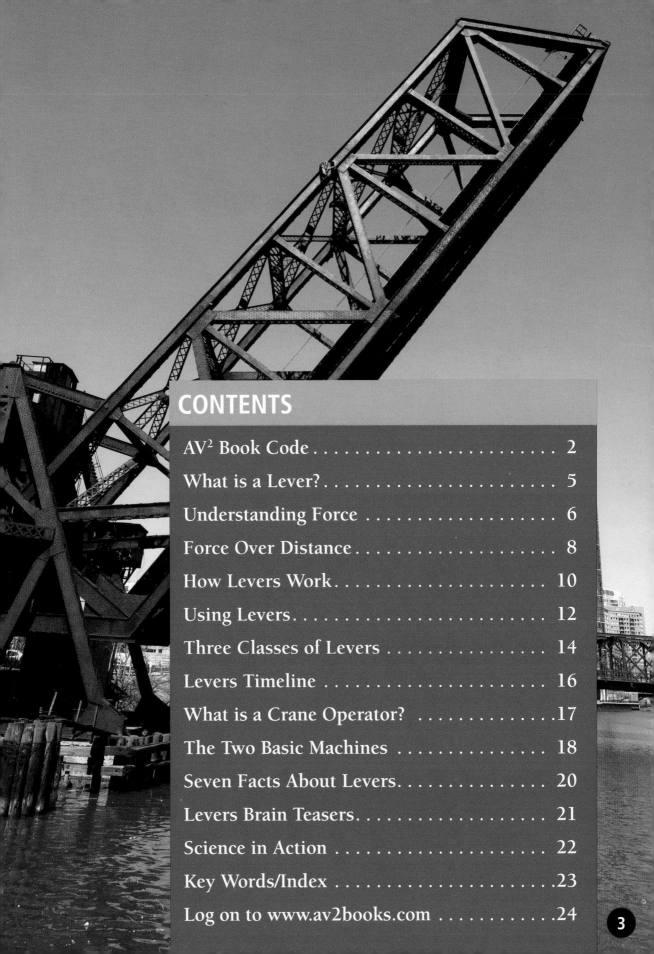

CONTENTS

A rake is a lever. People use rakes to remove leaves from lawns. When a person pulls a rake through leaves, the small movement of the hands pulling the handle is turned into a larger movement of the rake at the other end of the lever. In this way, using a rake makes it easier to move leaves than it would be without the rake.

What is a Lever?

A lever is a movable bar that rests on a solid point, called a **fulcrum**. Levers change the **effort** needed to move objects. People have used levers for thousands of years to help them push, pull, or lift objects. The word *lever* comes from a French word that means "to raise."

The lever is a simple machine. There are six simple machines, including the inclined plane, the pulley, the screw, the wedge, and the wheel and axle. All simple machines make work easier. They do not have batteries or motors. They do not add any **energy** of their own to help people do work. Instead, simple machines work by changing the forces that are applied to them.

■ A seesaw is a lever that makes it possible to lift a person off the ground on either end.

Understanding Force

Force is a push or a pull that causes an object to move or change its direction. When an object is not moving, or at rest, all of the forces pushing or pulling it are balanced. This balance is called **equilibrium**.

When scientists study forces and how objects move, there are three measurements they need to know. They must know the object's **weight**, how fast it is moving, and the amount of force that is causing the object to move. Understanding forces, how forces affect objects, and how objects affect each other can make it easier to move objects.

■ In a tug of war, each team applies force to the rope as they try to move the other team. If neither team is winning, the forces at each end of the rope are in equilibrium.

What is Gravity?

Gravity is a force that pulls one object toward another. All objects have some gravity, though it is often very weak. An object's gravity is related to its **mass**. The more mass an object has, the greater its force of gravity and the pull it creates. Earth is a massive object, which means it has a strong gravity. Earth's gravity pulls the objects on Earth toward the center of the planet.

Earth's gravity gives weight to an object's mass. A large rock has a great deal of mass. Earth's gravity pulls on this mass to create a heavy weight. A heavy weight needs a great force to make it move. This is why moving large objects often takes a great deal of effort.

MASS VS. WEIGHT

People often think mass and weight are the same, but they are very different. Mass is how much material an object contains. Weight is how strongly gravity pulls on an object. Mass is usually measured in kilograms, while weight is often measured in pounds.

A person with a mass of 91 kilograms weighs 200 pounds, but this is only true on Earth. This is because Earth's gravity pulls on a 91-kg mass with a force of 200 pounds. The Moon's much weaker gravity would only pull on a 91-kg mass with a force of 33 pounds. Also, if the person were to leave Earth on a space shuttle, he or she would become weightless. Even though the person would then weigh 0 pounds, his or her mass of 91 kg would not change.

Force Over Distance

In science, **work** happens when a force is used to move an object over a distance. For work to happen, the force that is applied must be in the same direction that the object is moving.

In other words, lifting a rock off the ground is work because the force applied to pull the rock up is going in the same upward direction that the rock is moving. On the other hand, holding a rock while walking is not work. This is because the forward movement of walking is not related to the upward force that is holding the rock up.

■ A pinball machine uses levers to keep the ball in play. When the ball is hit by the outside edge of a lever, it travels much farther than if the ball were hit by the inside edge.

As the force needed to move an object increases, the work involved in moving it also increases. This also applies to distance. The amount of work needed to move the object increases as the distance the object must move increases.

Simple machines make doing work easier. They do this by changing the amount and the direction of the force needed to move the object. Though less force is needed, simple machines require moving a greater distance.

CALCULATING WORK

The amount of work needed to lift a 10-pound (4.5-kg) ball changes based on the distance it is lifted. To calculate the work, the weight of the ball is multiplied by the height it will be moved.

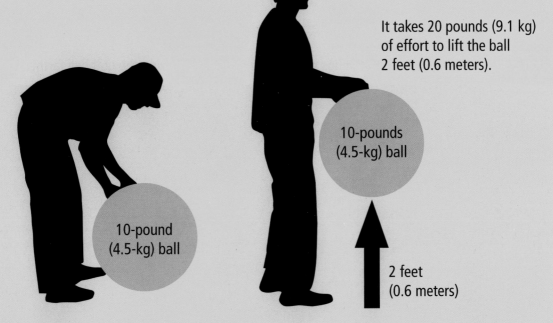

10 x 2 = 20

It takes 20 pounds (9.1 kg) of effort to lift the ball 2 feet (0.6 meters).

10-pounds (4.5-kg) ball

10-pound (4.5-kg) ball

2 feet (0.6 meters)

How Levers Work

Levers work by changing the amount and direction of a force. Using a lever offers a **mechanical advantage** that makes work easier. This means levers require less force to move an object than would be needed without a lever. This is because levers can increase force.

When placed on a fulcrum, a force may be applied to the long arm, or effort arm, of a lever. If the fulcrum is not in the center of the bar, this force is increased on the short arm, or **load** arm. The force on the effort arm is the input force. The force on the load arm is the output force. If the effort arm is made longer, the output force on the load arm is increased. In this way, a long lever can turn a small input force into a large output force.

However, the distance that the effort arm moves is much greater than the distance the load arm moves. This means that while a long lever increases the force applied to the load, it decreases the distance the load will be moved.

■ A golf club is a kind of lever. It magnifies the force of the swing, driving the golf ball farther.

CALCULATING EFFORT

A man using a lever to lift a 10-pound (4.5-kg) ball would find it easier to move the ball by making his end of the lever longer. Making the effort arm shorter, however, would mean that more force would be needed to move the ball.

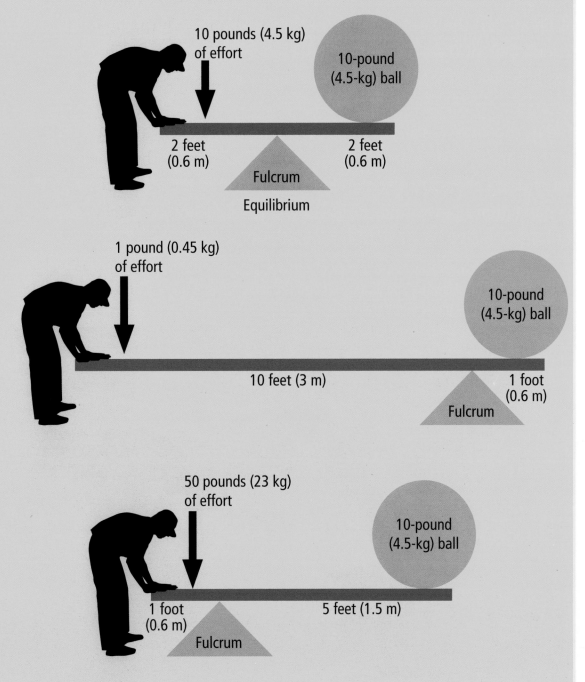

10 pounds (4.5 kg) of effort

10-pound (4.5-kg) ball

2 feet (0.6 m)

2 feet (0.6 m)

Fulcrum

Equilibrium

1 pound (0.45 kg) of effort

10-pound (4.5-kg) ball

10 feet (3 m)

1 foot (0.6 m)

Fulcrum

50 pounds (23 kg) of effort

10-pound (4.5-kg) ball

1 foot (0.6 m)

5 feet (1.5 m)

Fulcrum

Using Levers

The lever is one of the oldest machines used by humans. People used levers to build some of the world's best-known structures. Scientists believe ancient structures such as the Great Pyramid of Egypt and the Roman Colosseum were built with the help of levers. One of the oldest uses of the lever was the atlatl. This was a device early humans used to throw spears.

Today, the lever is still an important machine. Levers are used in their most basic forms, such as rakes and shovels, by people every day. Levers are also combined with other simple machines to make more powerful building tools, such as cranes, backhoes, and other heavy construction machines.

■ Each part of an excavator's long digging arm is connected at a fulcrum. This allows the arm to bend and move in different ways.

On the Salisbury Plain in England is a site called Stonehenge. Parts of it are more than 5,000 years old. The most well-known feature of Stonehenge is a ring of very large stones. **Archaeologists** believe people brought these giant stones from Wales. That is a distance of 160 miles (257 kilometers). Some of the stones weigh more than 44 tons (40 metric tons).

People needed a way to lift these massive stones into place. To move such large stones, archaeologists believe one of the tools used must have been the lever. Such levers were likely long tree trunks, with large stones used as fulcrums. Using these simple levers, people moved the heavy stones into upright positions.

Three Classes of Levers

A lever can be set up in three different ways in relation to its fulcrum. Each way may operate differently, but the concept is the same. Each type of lever magnifies the input force to make work easier.

FIRST-CLASS LEVER

A first-class lever has the fulcrum in the middle of the bar. The load and effort are at opposite ends of the bar. A seesaw is an example of a first-class lever.

SECOND-CLASS LEVER

A second-class lever has the fulcrum at the end of the bar. The load is in the middle of the bar, and the effort is at the opposite end. A wheelbarrow is an example of a second-class lever.

THIRD-CLASS LEVER

A third-class lever has the fulcrum at the end of the bar. The effort is in the middle of the bar, and the load is at the opposite end. A fishing rod is an example of a third class lever. The fisherman's end is the fulcrum, while the fish is the load.

Levers in Action

Every day, people around the world use levers in many different ways.

HAMMER CLAW

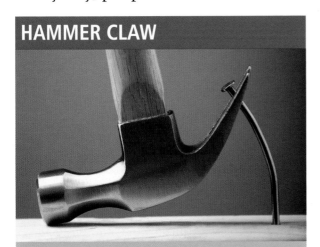

The claw of a hammer is a first-class lever. It is used to pull nails out of boards. The hammer head acts as a fulcrum, and the claw pulls the nail upward when force is applied to the handle.

BASEBALL BAT

A baseball bat is a third-class lever. One hand becomes the fulcrum when the bat is swung. The other hand provides the input force of the swing. When the bat hits a ball, the ball becomes the load to be moved.

NUTCRACKER

A nutcracker is two second-class levers. The fulcrum is the hinge that joins the two levers. A squeezing force applied to the ends of the handles is magnified on the nut, which is the load.

CAR DOOR

A car door is a second-class lever. The fulcrum is the hinge that joins the door to the car. The door itself is the load. The effort is applied to the handle near the edge of the door.

Levers Timeline

15,000 BC 5000 BC 3000 BC 2700 BC 400 BC 300 BC 200 BC 100 BC 1 AD 100 1900 1950 2000

1 **15,000 BC**
The atlatl is invented. This machine uses a lever to help a person throw a spear much farther than would be possible without the atlatl.

2 **5000 BC**
Levers are used to weigh items, such as grapes.

3 **3000 BC**
The building of Stonehenge begins. Over the next 1,500 years, several large, stone monuments are built.

4 **2700 BC**
The Egyptians begin to build pyramids. Most scientists believe they used levers to do so.

5 **400 BC**
The ancient Greek, Dionysius of Syracuse, invents the catapult.

6 **250 BC**
Archimedes discovers the law of equilibrium.

7 **100 AD**
Romans invent scissors that have two levers connected at a fulcrum. Another kind of scissor was in use earlier, but it was of a different design.

8 **1894**
William Chauncey Hooker invents the mousetrap. It uses levers to snap shut and catch the mouse.

9 **1908**
The first tower cranes made for the construction industry are introduced.

10 **2009**
Taisun, the world's strongest crane, is built. It can lift a weight of about 22,000 tons (20,000 metric tons).

What is a Crane Operator?

There are many kinds of cranes, and they operate in different ways. Crane operators learn how to use these different cranes to move heavy objects. The cranes may be mobile, such as on the back of a truck, or fixed in place. Fixed cranes can be very large. They are used to lift very heavy objects, often high into the air. Crane operators must have training before they can operate a crane. They must learn how levers work and how they can be used to safely move large or heavy objects.

■ The Burj Khalifa is the tallest building in the world, at 2,722 feet (830 m). Cranes lifted 69,446 tons (63,000 metric tons) of equipment to build the 163-floor structure.

Archimedes

Archimedes was an ancient Greek inventor and **engineer**. He was born in the city of Syracuse in 287 BC. Archimedes is famous for his many discoveries and inventions. Among his many accomplishments, Archimedes is known for explaining how levers work. Based on his study of levers, Archimedes is reported to have said, "Give me a place to stand on, and I will move the Earth."

The Two Basic Machines

The inclined plane and the lever are the most basic of all simple machines. In fact, all six simple machines can be seen as one of these two most basic machines.

TYPES OF INCLINED PLANE

The inclined plane is the simplest of the simple machines. Any slope, such as a hill, is an inclined plane.

A wedge is two inclined planes put together.

A screw is an inclined plane wrapped around a center bar.

TYPES OF LEVERS

A lever is a bar that rests on a pivot, or fulcrum. Pushing down on one end of the bar helps to lift a load on the other end of the bar.

A wheel and axle is a lever in which the bar circles around the fulcrum, or axle.

A pulley is a lever that uses a wheel for a fulcrum and a rope instead of a bar.

Complex Machines

Simple machines can be combined to make other kinds of machines. When two simple machines are combined, this new machine is often called a compound or complex machine. Levers can be used together with other simple machines to create useful devices.

CLOTHESPIN

A clothespin is a lever that makes it possible to hang heavy clothes to dry. A clothespin uses two movable inclined planes that are attached at the fulcrum.

SCISSORS

Scissors use two movable levers to cut material. A screw connects two inclined planes at the fulcrum. Squeezing the handles moves both of the blades together. The blades act as wedges to cut material.

FORKLIFT

Forklifts and other heavy machines often use levers, pulleys, and wheels and axles to make the work of moving large or heavy objects easier.

Seven Facts About Levers

The human arm is a lever. The elbow is the fulcrum, and the bicep is the effort.

In order to set off a fire alarm, the lever must first be pulled.

Piano keys are long levers that work with other simple machines to make sound.

A bottle opener is a lever. The fulcrum rests on top of the cap, while the hand creates the effort.

The gear stick in a car or truck is a lever that allows the driver to change gears.

Dogs are trained to use levers like the seesaw. This demonstrates their skills at dog shows.

Foosball tables use levers to move the ball.

Levers Brain Teasers

1 What does a lever do?

2 Where is the fulcrum placed in a first-class lever?

3 Where is the load placed in a second-class lever?

4 Where is the effort placed in a third-class lever?

5 Who is known for first explaining how levers work?

6 When was Stonehenge built?

7 How many simple machines are there?

8 Name one example of a third-class lever.

9 What modern building machines use levers?

10 Who was Archimedes?

Science in Action

Build a First-class Lever

Learn more about motion and how the fulcrum affects the force needed to move a lever.

Materials Needed

eraser

heavy stone, no larger than 3 inches (7.6 centimeters)

ruler

tape

Directions

1 Begin by taping the rock to the top of one end of the ruler. The rock is the load that will be moved.

2 Next, put the eraser on the table. This will be the fulcrum.

3 Place the ruler on top of the eraser. The eraser should be under the center of the ruler.

4 Push down on the end of the ruler opposite the rock. Notice how much you had to push to raise the rock off the table.

5 Now, move the fulcrum closer to the end of the ruler that has the rock, and push down again. Notice how much force is needed and how far the rock moves.

6 Finally, put the fulcrum closer to the end of the ruler that does not have the rock. Push down, and notice how much force is needed to push the ruler.

Key Words

archaeologists: scientists who study the remains of old cultures

effort: the amount of work it takes to move an object

energy: power needed to do work

engineer: a person who designs structures or machines, often using knowledge of simple machines

equilibrium: a state when all the forces acting on an object are balanced

fulcrum: the point where a lever turns

load: the object or substance being worked on by a simple machine

mass: a measure of the amount of matter an object contains

mechanical advantage: the amount of force produced by an object compared to how much is applied to the object

weight: the force of gravity's pull on an object's mass

work: force applied over distance to move an object

Index

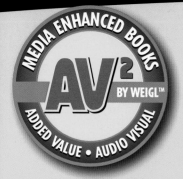

Log on to www.av2books.com

AV² by Weigl brings you media enhanced books that support active learning. Go to www.av2books.com, and enter the special code found on page 2 of this book. You will gain access to enriched and enhanced content that supplements and complements this book. Content includes video, audio, weblinks, quizzes, a slide show, and activities.

AV² Online Navigation

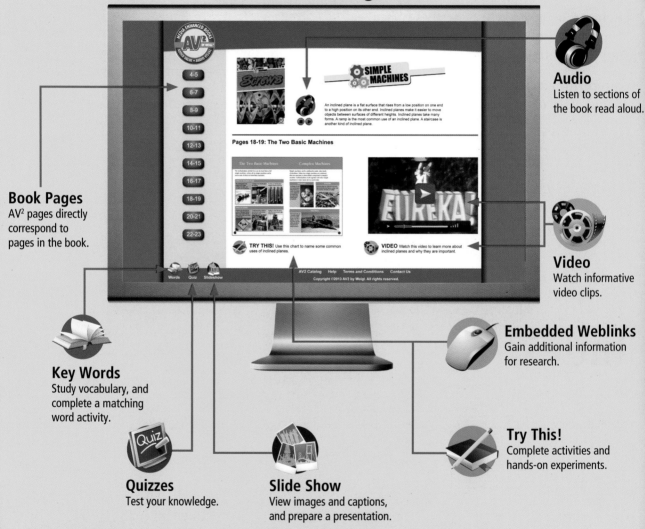

Book Pages
AV² pages directly correspond to pages in the book.

Key Words
Study vocabulary, and complete a matching word activity.

Quizzes
Test your knowledge.

Slide Show
View images and captions, and prepare a presentation.

Audio
Listen to sections of the book read aloud.

Video
Watch informative video clips.

Embedded Weblinks
Gain additional information for research.

Try This!
Complete activities and hands-on experiments.

AV² was built to bridge the gap between print and digital. We encourage you to tell us what you like and what you want to see in the future.

Sign up to be an AV² Ambassador at www.av2books.com/ambassador.

Due to the dynamic nature of the Internet, some of the URLs and activities provided as part of AV² by Weigl may have changed or ceased to exist. AV² by Weigl accepts no responsibility for any such changes. All media enhanced books are regularly monitored to update addresses and sites in a timely manner. Contact AV² by Weigl at 1-866-649-3445 or av2books@weigl.com with any questions, comments, or feedback.